Let the wil hear you

Elisabeth Contreras-Moran

Text copyright © Elisabeth Contreras-Moran, 2021
Illustrations copyright © Elisabeth Contreras-Moran, 2021

All rights reserved. No part of this book may be reproduced or used in any manner without the express written permission of the copyright owner except for the use of quotations in a book review.

for all adventurers, who do not wish to hurry but instead meander and observe, especially my own dearest child, Jack, who reminds me daily of the magic of nature experienced in childhood (and beyond for those lucky few)

and

for those who adventured farther than the eye can see, into the great Beyond, especially Joaquin, Jim and Bob Contreras. I miss you all so very much but am so grateful for how often I find your memories in nature.

With special thanks to Sandra Spiess, Marta Yahner and Ileana LaFontaine for their edits, advice and encouragement. Hey Mom, is your daughter a real author yet?

Dearest child, did you know?

The wild can hear you.

May the first signs of spring remind you to believe in new beginnings. Always.

May you choose to explore many pathless routes through greenly scented woodlands.

May you share stories with every leaf, rock stick and insect you meet along the way.

May the summer bumblebee teach you the impossible, magical physics of flying.

Printed in Great Britain
by Amazon

Dearest child, may you remember; the wild can hear you.

Let it. Let the wild hear you.

may a pebble, a feather, a shell forever fit in your pocket as a touchstone of your wild.

And always, always, no matter the season, may your heart soar outdoors to play with wild abandon and may your soul feel the reverberations of nature through your bare toes rooted in the soil and

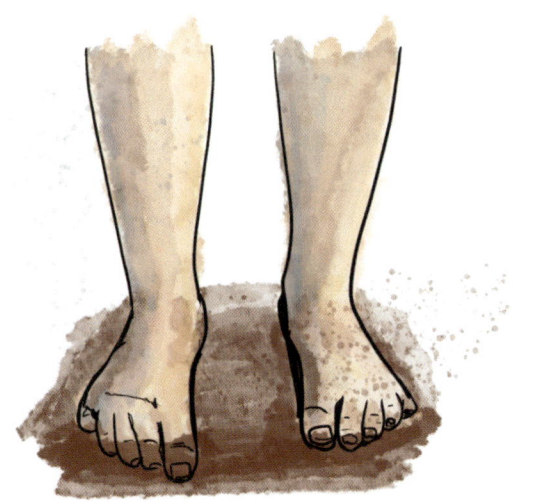

May a sunrise show you hope while a sunset shows you not to fear the shadows.

May you yell your wild into the depths of a sudden storm.

May the icy breaths of winter sparkle into your unlimited imagination.

May you climb a hill just so the wind can play with your hair while you two howl together.

May you discover gentleness amongst the most fragile of the foliage.

May the early signs of autumn show you how
to fall, but also how to get back up.

May you quietly whisper your thoughts to the hushed cadence of the creek.

May you greet the bird and squirrel with your own singing, chattering voice in return for theirs.